THE BIBLE

THE OLD TESTAMENT
GENESIS

PART 1

ADAPTATION
Jean-Christophe Camus ~ Michel Dufranne

DESIGN AND COLORS
Damir Zitko

COLORS
Vladimir Mario Davidenko

Adaptation based on the translation of Louis the Second (1901).
All the stories are faithful to the translation.

HEAVY METAL

2008- GUY DELCOURT PROUDCTIONS- CAMUS- DUFRANNE- ZITKO
THE BIBLE
ISBN 978-1935351-20-7
PUBLISHED BY HEAVY METAL
100 NORTH VILLAGE AVENUE
SUITE 12
ROCKVILLE CENTRE, NY 11570

PRINTED IN CHINA

FOREWORD

The Bible remains the most widely available book in the World, but who among us has read it entirely through? At once a literary juggernaut, one of the staples of our civilization and a holy book for Christians and Jews alike, the Bible proves to be a demanding read; a complexity that stems from its variegated nature. It is indeed a collection of very diverse book genres—poems, myths, historical tales, prayers and ritualistic codes—that had been written throughout different ages and were assembled shortly before our present era into one collected volume. The word "Bible" actually ought to be pluralized. It derives from Byblos, which was a type of papyrus the Greeks had named after the Phoenician city that manufactured it. The plural "ta biblia" (books) was subsequently used to describe the Jewish holy book, in reference to the numerous scrolls that composed it. Near the beginning of our era the first Christian communities would start integrating Greek translations of the Hebrew bible into the canon of their own sacred texts, while simultaneously adding some of their own tales. One such instance would be the four gospels relating the life and teachings of Jesus. Later, the Christians would divide their bible into two main sections, the Old Testament (the Jewish bible) and the New Testament (the Christian writings).

But the Bible is nowadays more than just the holy book of the Jewish and Christian communities. It lies at the very root of our whole western civilization. Even the Muslim culutre derives from it, for not only was the prophet Mohammad a direct descendant of the children of Abraham, but the Koran also clearly features several biblical events. Be one Jewish, Christian or Muslim, believer or non-believer, it proves invaluable to be familiar with the Bible in order to understand the roots of our history, and the beliefs and myths that crafted it. I therefore enthusiastically welcome the publication of this bible, presented in a graphic novel format that will make major biblical stories accessible to all. This project is focused on the preeminent and most meaningful chapters, starting with the famous story of Genesis that describes the covenant between God and Man. The panel layouts are strong, both faithful to the story and pleasant to read, while the line work is clear, precise and subtly implies the Eastern and poetic character of the texts. Let me also add that the French translation chosen by the authors for the original text is that of Louis the Second, one of the best and most faithful to the Hebrew text.

Frederic Lenoir
Philosopher and director of the magazine "Le Monde des Religions"

IN THE BEGINNING, GOD CREATED THE HEAVENS AND THE EARTH. THE EARTH WAS A FORMLESS AND EMPTY VOID. DARKNESS COVERED THE FACE OF THE DEEP, AND GOD'S SPIRIT SWEPT OVER THE FACE OF THE WATERS. GOD SAID:

"LET THERE BE LIGHT!"

FIRST DAY.

"LET THERE BE A DOME IN THE MIDST OF THE WATERS, AND LET IT SEPARATE THE WATERS FROM THE WATERS."

SECOND DAY.

"LET THE WATERS UNDER THE SKY BE GATHERED TOGETHER INTO ONE PLACE, AND LET THE DRY LAND APPEAR."

"LET THE EARTH PUT FORTH VEGETATION; PLANTS YIELDING SEED, AND FRUIT TREES OF EVERY KIND ON EARTH THAT BEAR FRUIT WITH THE SEED IN IT."

THIRD DAY.

"LET THERE BE LIGHTS IN THE DOME OF THE SKY TO SEPARATE THE DAY FROM THE NIGHT; AND LET THEM BE FOR SIGNS AND FOR SEASONS AND FOR DAYS AND YEARS, AND LET THEM BE LIGHTS IN THE DOME OF THE SKY TO GIVE LIGHT UPON THE EARTH."

FOURTH DAY.

"LET THE WATERS BRING FORTH SWARMS OF LIVING CREATURES, AND LET BIRDS FLY ABOVE THE EARTH ACROSS THE DOME OF THE SKY."

"BE FRUITFUL AND MULTIPLY AND FILL THE WATERS IN THE SEAS, AND LET BIRDS MULTIPLY ON THE EARTH."

FIFTH DAY.

"LET THE EARTH BRING FORTH LIVING CREATURES OF EVERY KIND: CATTLE AND CREEPING THINGS AND WILD ANIMALS OF THE EARTH OF EVERY KIND."

"LET US MAKE HUMANKIND IN OUR IMAGE, ACCORDING TO OUR LIKENESS; AND LET THEM HAVE DOMINION OVER THE FISH OF THE SEA, AND OVER THE BIRDS OF THE AIR, AND OVER THE CATTLE, AND OVER EVERY CREEPING THING THAT CREEPS UPON THE EARTH."

"BE FRUITFUL AND MULTIPLY, AND FILL THE EARTH AND SUBDUE IT; AND HAVE DOMINION OVER THE FISH OF THE SEA AND OVER THE BIRDS OF THE AIR AND OVER EVERY LIVING THING THAT MOVES UPON THE EARTH."

"SEE, I HAVE GIVEN YOU EVERY PLANT YIELDING SEED THAT IS UPON THE FACE OF ALL THE EARTH, AND EVERY TREE WITH SEED IN ITS FRUIT; YOU SHALL HAVE THEM FOR FOOD. AND TO EVERY BEAST OF THE EARTH AND TO EVERY BIRD OF THE AIR, AND TO EVERYTHING THAT CREEPS ON THE EARTH, EVERYTHING THAT HAS THE BREATH OF LIFE, I HAVE GIVEN EVERY GREEN PLANT FOR FOOD."

SIXTH DAY.

SEVENTH DAY.

THE LORD GOD PLANTED A GARDEN IN EDEN, IN THE EAST; AND THERE HE PUT THE MAN WHOM HE HAD FORMED. OUT OF THE GROUND THE LORD GOD MADE TO GROW EVERY TREE THAT IS PLEASANT TO THE SIGHT AND GOOD FOR FOOD, THE TREE OF LIFE ALSO IN THE MIDST OF THE GARDEN, AND THE TREE OF KNOWLEDGE OF GOOD AND EVIL.

A RIVER FLOWED OUT OF EDEN TO WATER THE GARDEN, AND FROM THERE IT DIVIDED AND BECAME FOUR BRANCHES. THE NAME OF THE FIRST IS PISHON; IT IS THE ONE THAT FLOWS AROUND THE WHOLE LAND OF HAVILAH, WHERE THERE IS GOLD.

THE NAME OF THE SECOND RIVER IS GIHON; IT IS THE ONE THAT FLOWS AROUND THE WHOLE LAND OF CUSH.

THE LORD GOD TOOK THE MAN AND PUT HIM IN THE GARDEN OF EDEN TO TILL IT AND KEEP IT.

"YOU MAY FREELY EAT OF EVERY TREE OF THE GARDEN; BUT OF THE TREE OF KNOWLEDGE OF GOOD AND EVIL YOU SHALL NOT EAT, FOR IN THE DAY THAT YOU EAT OF IT YOU SHALL DIE."

THE NAME OF THE THIRD RIVER IS TIGRIS, WHICH FLOWS EAST OF ASSYRIA.

AND THE FOURTH RIVER IS THE EUPHRATES.

"IT IS NOT GOOD THAT THE MAN SHOULD BE ALONE, I WILL MAKE HIM A HELPER AS HIS PARTNER."

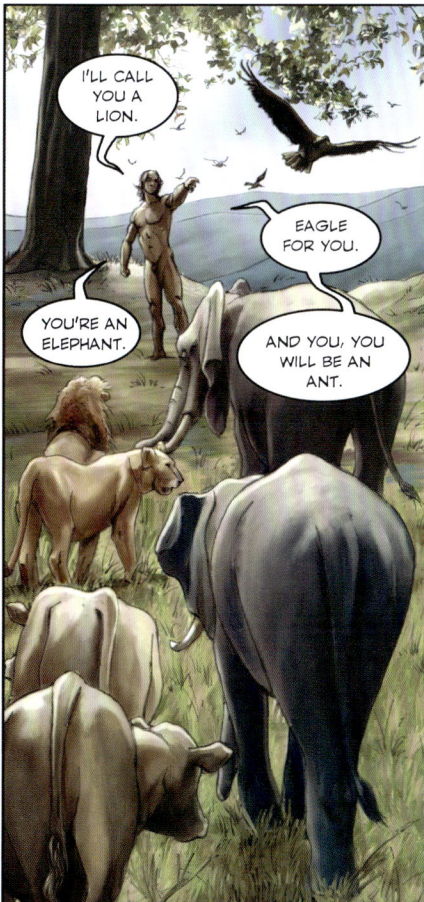

I'LL CALL YOU A LION.

EAGLE FOR YOU.

YOU'RE AN ELEPHANT.

AND YOU, YOU WILL BE AN ANT.

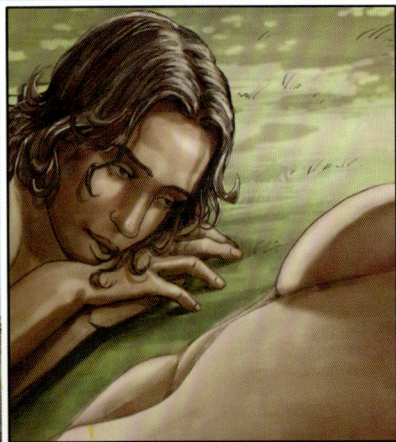

THIS AT LAST IS BONE OF MY
BONES AND FLESH OF MY FLESH;
THIS ONE SHALL BE CALLED
WOMAN, FOR OUT OF MAN THIS
ONE WAS TAKEN.

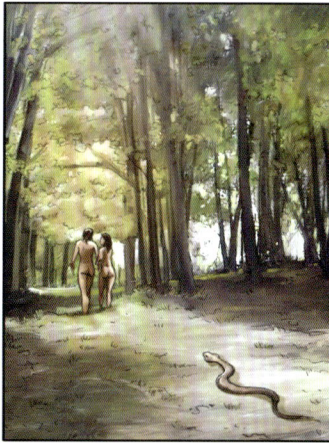

WHO ARE YOU?

THEY SAY I'M A "SNAKE".

IS IT TRUE THAT GOD SAID: YOU SHALL NOT EAT FROM ANY TREE IN THE GARDEN?

WE MAY EAT THE FRUIT OF THE TREES IN THE GARDEN...

... BUT GOD SAID: YOU SHALL NOT OF THE FRUIT OF THE TREE THAT IS IN THE MIDDLE OF THE GARDEN, NOR TOUCH IT OR YOU SHALL DIE.

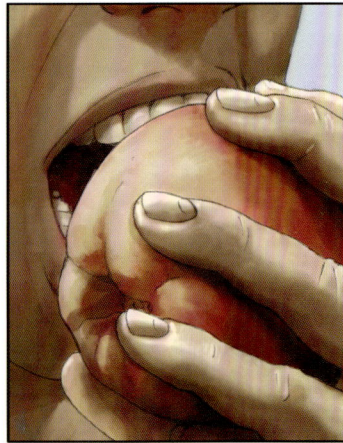

"WHERE ARE YOU?"

"I HEARD YOUR VOICE IN THE GARDEN, LORD.

"I WAS AFRAID, BECAUSE I WAS NAKED; AND I HID MYSELF!

"WHO TOLD YOU THAT YOU WERE NAKED? HAVE YOU EATEN FROM THE TREE OF WHICH I COMMANDED YOU NOT TO EAT?"

THE WOMAN, SHE GAVE ME FRUIT FROM THE TREE... AND I ATE IT!

"WHY DID YOU DO THAT?"

THE SERPENT TRICKED ME, AND I ATE.

"BECAUSE YOU HAVE DONE THIS, CURSED ARE YOU AMONG ALL ANIMALS AND AMONG ALL WILD CREATURES; UPON YOUR BELLY YOU SHALL GO, AND DUST SHALL EAT ALL THE DAYS OF YOUR LIFE. I WILL PUT ETERNITY BETWEEN YOU AND THE WOMAN, AND BETWEEN YOUR OFFSPRING AND HERS; HE WILL STRIKE YOUR HEAD, AND YOU WILL STRIKE HIS HEEL."

"I WILL GREATLY INCREASE YOUR PANGS IN CHILDBEARING, IN PAIN YOU SHALL BRING FORTH CHILDREN, YET YOUR DESIRE SHALL BE FOR YOUR HUSBAND, AND HE SHALL RULE OVER YOU."

"BECAUSE YOU HAVE LISTENED TO THE VOICE OF YOUR WIFE, CURSED IS THE GROUND BECAUSE OF YOU; IN TOIL YOU SHALL EAT OF IT ALL THE DAYS OF YOUR LIFE; THORNS AND THISTLES IT SHALL BRING FORTH FOR YOU; AND YOU SHALL EAT THE PLANTS OF THE FIELD."

THE MAN NAMED HIS WIFE EVE.

"BY THE SWEAT OF YOUR FACE YOU SHALL EAT BREAD UNTIL YOU RETURN TO THE GROUND, FOR OUT OF IT YOU WERE TAKEN; YOU ARE DUST, AND TO DUST YOU SHALL RETURN."

THE MAN INTIMATELY KNEW HIS WIFE EVE.

SHE CONCEIVED AND BORE CAIN.

NEXT SHE BORE HIS BROTHER ABEL.

ABEL WAS A KEEPER OF SHEEP...

... AND CAIN A TILLER OF THE GROUND.

O LORD, PLEASE ACCEPT THESE THREE YOUNG SHEEP AS AN OFFERING.

AS WELL AS THESE FRUIT AND VEGETABLES FROM THE EARTH.

THE LORD HAS REGARD FOR ABEL AND HIS OFFERING...

BUT FOR CAIN AND HIS OFFERING HE HAD NO REGARD.

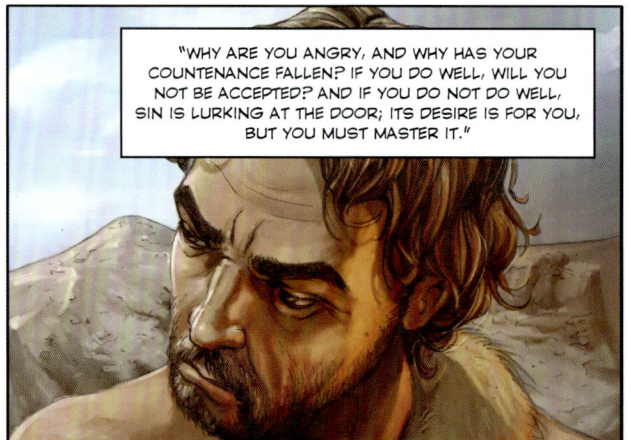

"WHY ARE YOU ANGRY, AND WHY HAS YOUR COUNTENANCE FALLEN? IF YOU DO WELL, WILL YOU NOT BE ACCEPTED? AND IF YOU DO NOT DO WELL, SIN IS LURKING AT THE DOOR; ITS DESIRE IS FOR YOU, BUT YOU MUST MASTER IT."

ABEL, MY BROTHER, I NEED TO SPEAK WITH YOU. LET'S SIT HERE.

CAIN, WHAT IS SO IMPORTANT?

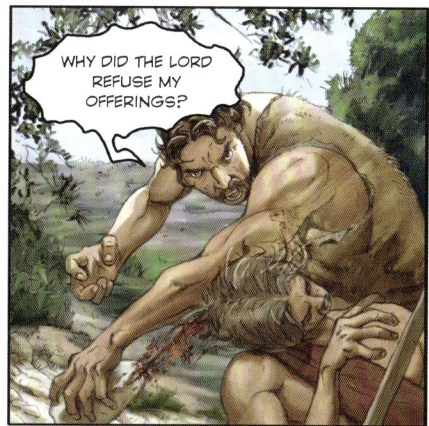

WHY DID THE LORD REFUSE MY OFFERINGS?

WHY? WHY? WHY?

"WHERE IS YOUR BROTHER ABEL?"

I DO NOT KNOW!

I'M NOT MY BROTHER'S KEEPER!

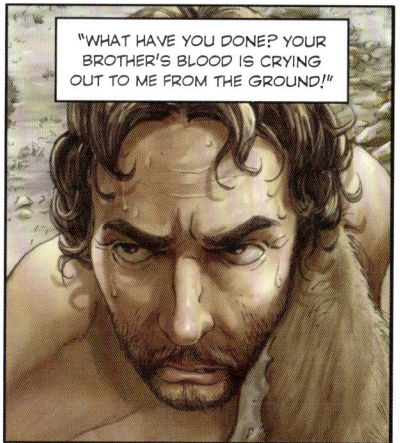

"WHAT HAVE YOU DONE? YOUR BROTHER'S BLOOD IS CRYING OUT TO ME FROM THE GROUND!"

"AND NOW YOU WILL BE CURSED FROM THE GROUND, WHICH HAS OPENED ITS MOUTH TO RECEIVE YOUR BROTHER'S BLOOD FROM YOUR HAND. WHEN YOU TILL THE GROUND, IT WILL NO LONGER YIELD TO YOU ITS STRENGTH; YOU WILL BE A FUGITIVE AND A WANDERER ON THE EARTH."

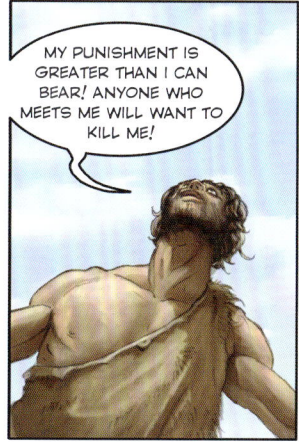

MY PUNISHMENT IS GREATER THAN I CAN BEAR! ANYONE WHO MEETS ME WILL WANT TO KILL ME!

"WHOEVER KILLS CAIN WILL SUFFER A SEVENFOLD VENGEANCE!"

AND THE LORD PUT A MARK ON CAIN, SO THAT NO ONE WHO CAME UPON HIM WOULD KILL HIM. THEN CAIN WENT AWAY FROM THE PRESENCE OF THE LORD, AND SETTLED IN THE LAND OF NOD, EAST OF EDEN.

WHEN PEOPLE BEGAN TO MULTIPLY ON THE FACE OF THE GROUND, AND DAUGHTERS WERE BORN TO THEM, THE SONS OF GOD SAW THAT THEY WERE FAIR; AND THEY TOOK WIVES FOR THEMSELVES OF ALL THAT THEY CHOSE.

GENESIS 6-1

THE LORD SAW THAT THE WICKEDNESS OF HUMANKIND WAS GREAT IN THE EARTH, AND THAT EVERY INCLINATION OF THE THOUGHTS OF THEIR HEARTS WAS ONLY EVIL CONTINUALLY.

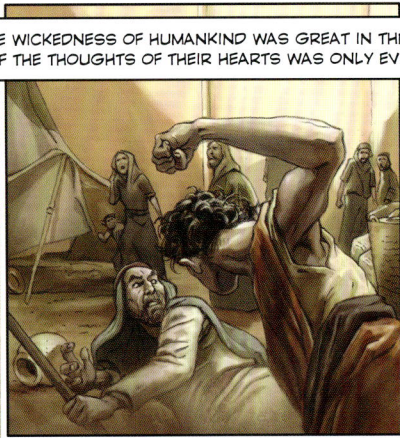

"I WILL BLOT OUT FROM THE EARTH THE HUMAN BEINGS I HAVE CREATED- PEOPLE TOGETHER WITH ANIMALS AND CREEPING THINGS AND BIRDS OF THE AIR, FOR I AM SORRY THAT I HAVE MADE THEM."

BUT NOAH FOUND FAVOR IN THE SIGHT OF THE LORD. NOAH WAS A KIND AND RIGHTEOUS MAN: NOAH WALKED WITH THE LORD.

"I HAVE DETERMINED TO MAKED AN END OF ALL FLESH, FOR THE EARTH IS FILLED WITH VIOLENCE BECAUSE OF THEM; NOW I AM GOING TO DESTROY THEM ALONG WITH THE EARTH."

"MAKE YOURSELF AN ARK OF CYPRESS WOOD."

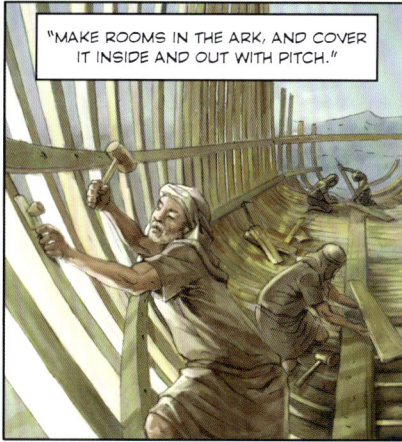

"MAKE ROOMS IN THE ARK, AND COVER IT INSIDE AND OUT WITH PITCH."

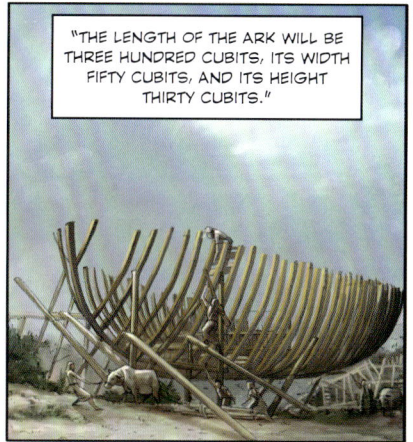

"THE LENGTH OF THE ARK WILL BE THREE HUNDRED CUBITS, ITS WIDTH FIFTY CUBITS, AND ITS HEIGHT THIRTY CUBITS."

"MAKE A WINDOW FOR THE ARK, AND FINISH IT TO A CUBIT ABOVE; AND PUT THE DOOR OF THE ARK IN ITS SIDE; MAKE IT WITH LOWER, SECOND, AND THIRD DECKS."

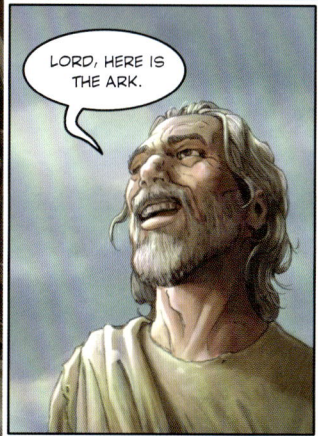

LORD, HERE IS THE ARK.

"I AM GOING TO BRING A FLOOD OF WATERS ON THE EARTH, TO DESTROY FROM UNDER HEAVEN ALL FLESH IN WHICH IS THE BREATH OF LIFE; EVERYTHING THAT IS ON THE EARTH SHALL DIE."

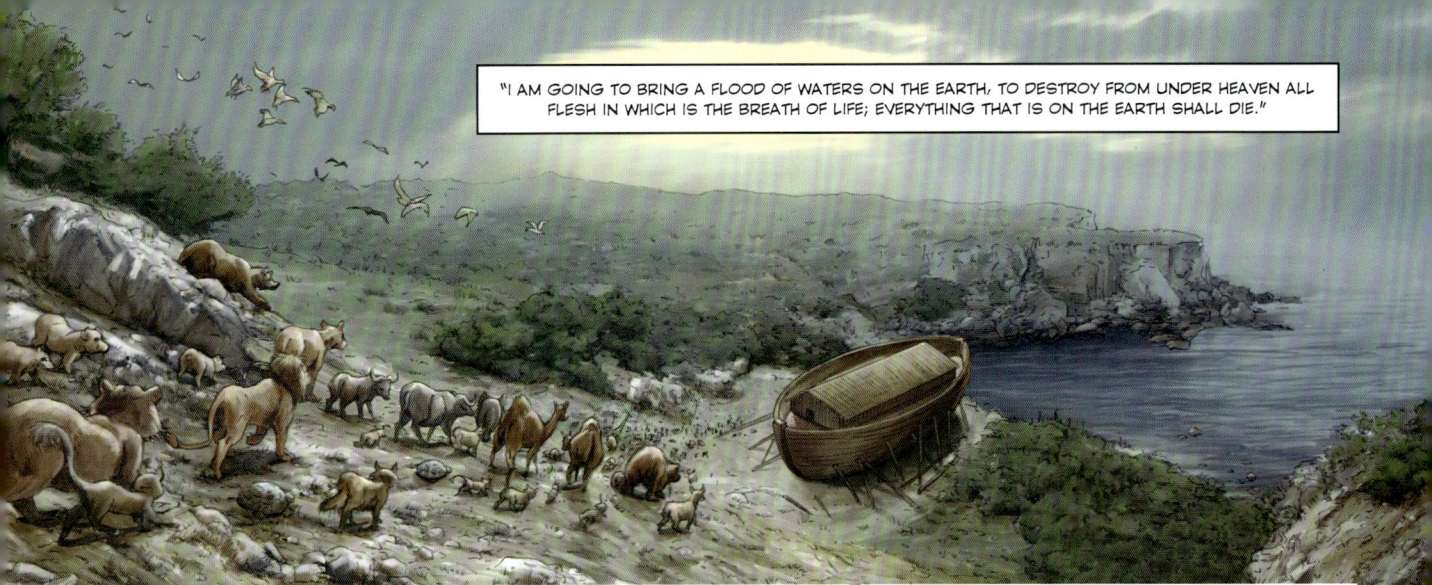

"YOU SHALL COME INTO THE ARK, YOU, YOUR SONS, YOUR WIFE, AND YOUR SONS' WIVES WITH YOU."

"AND OF EVERY LIVING THING, OF ALL FLESH, YOU SHALL BRING TWO OF EVERY KIND INTO THE ARK."

"BIRDS ACCORDING TO THEIR KINDS, LIVESTOCK ACCORDING TO THEIR KINDS."

"EVERY CREEPING THING OF THE GROUND ACCORDING TO ITS KIND."

"TAKE WITH YOU EVERY KIND OF FOOD THAT IS EATEN, AND STORE IT UP; AND IT SHALL SERVE AS FOOD FOR YOU AND FOR THEM."

NOAH, HE DID ALL THAT GOD COMMANDED HIM.

SEVEN DAYS LATER, THE WATER OF
FLOODS WAS UPON THE EARTH.

THE FLOOD CONTINUED FOR FORTY DAYS ON THE EARTH.

AND ALL THE FLESH DIED THAT MOVED ON THE EARTH. ONLY NOAH WAS LEFT, AND THOSE THAT WERE WITH HIM IN THE ARK.

AND THE WATERS SWELLED ON THE EARTH FOR ONE HUNDRED AND FIFTY DAYS.

THE FOUNTAINS OF THE DEEP AND THE WINDOWS OF THE HEAVENS WERE CLOSED; THE RAIN FROM THE HEAVENS ENDED. THE WATERS GRADUALLY RECEDED FROM THE EARTH. AT THE END OF ONE HUNDRED AND FIFTY DAYS THE WATERS HAD ABATED. IN THE SEVENTH MONTH, ON THE SEVENTEENTH DAY OF THE MONTH, THE ARK CAME TO REST ON THE MOUNTAINS OF ARARAT.

IN THE TENTH MONTH, ON THE FIRST DAY OF THE MONTH, THE TOPS OF THE MOUNTAINS APPEARED.

AT THE END OF FOURTY DAYS NOAH OPENED THE WINDOW OF THE ARK THAT HE HAD MADE.

IF YOU COME BACK, IT MEANS THE WATERS ARE COVERING THE EARTH.

HE SENT OUT THE RAVEN; AND IT WENT TO AND FRO UNTIL THE WATERS WERE DRIED UP FROM THE EARTH. THEN HE SENT OUT THE DOVE FROM HIM, TO SEE IF THE WATERS HAD SUBSIDED FROM THE FACE OF THE GROUND.

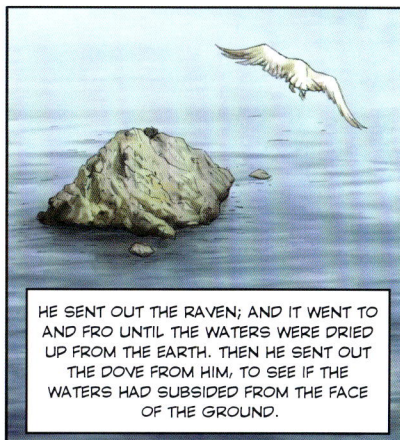

HE WAITED ANOTHER SEVEN DAYS, AND AGAIN HE SENT OUT THE DOVE FROM THE ARK; AND THE DOVE CAME BACK TO HIM IN THE EVENING, AND THERE IN ITS BEAK WAS A FRESHLY PLUCKED OLIVE LEAF.

THE WATERS HAD FINALLY GONE DOWN..

THEN HE WAITED ANOTHER SEVEN DAYS, AND SENT OUT THE DOVE; AND IT DID NOT RETURN TO HIM ANYMORE. IN THE SIX HUNDRED AND FIRST YEAR, IN THE FIRST MONTH, ON THE FIRST DAY OF THE MONTH, THE WATERS WERE DRIED UP FROM THE EARTH.

IN THE SECOND MONTH, ON THE TWENTY-SEVENTH DAY OF THE MONTH, THE EARTH WAS DRY.

THEN GOD SAID TO NOAH, GO OUT OF THE ARK, YOU AND YOUR WIFE, AND YOUR SONS AND YOUR SONS' WIVES WITH YOU.

"BRING OUT WITH YOU EVERY LIVING THING THAT IS WITH YOU OF ALL FLESH– SO THAT THEY MAY ABOUND ON THE EARTH, AND BE FRUITFUL AND MULTIPLY ON THE EARTH."

THEN NOAH BUILT AN ALTAR TO THE LORD, AND TOOK OF EVERY CLEAN ANIMAL AND OF EVERY CLEAN BIRD, AND OFFERED BURNT-OFFERINGS OF THE ALTAR.

"I WILL NEVER AGAIN CURSE THE GROUND BECAUSE OF HUMANKIND, FOR THE INCLINATION OF THE HUMAN HEART IS EVIL FROM YOUTH; NOR WILL I EVER DESTROY EVERY LIVING CREATURE AS I HAVE DONE."

"AS LONG AS THE EARTH ENDURES, SEEDTIME AND HARVEST, COLD AND HEAT..."

"... SUMMER AND WINTER, DAY AND NIGHT, SHALL NOT CEASE!"

"BE FRUITFUL AND MULTIPLY, AND FILL THE EARTH."

EVERY MOVING THING THAT LIVES SHALL BE FOOD FOR YOU; AND JUST AS I GAVE YOU THE GREEN PLANTS, I GIVE YOU EVERYTHING.

"WHOEVER SHEDS THE BLOOD OF A HUMAN, BY A HUMAN SHALL THAT PERSON'S BLOOD BE SHED; FOR IN HIS OWN IMAGE GOD MADE HUMANKIND."

"I ESTABLISH MY COVENANT WITH YOU, THAT NEVER AGAIN SHALL ALL FLESH BE CUT OFF BY THE WATERS OF A FLOOD, AND NEVER AGAIN SHALL THERE BE A FLOOD TO DESTORY THE EARTH."

"THIS IS THE SIGN OF THE COVENANT THAT I MAKE BETWEEN ME AND YOU AND EVERY LIVING CREATURE THAT IS WITH YOU, FOR ALL FUTURE GENERATIONS: I HAVE SET MY BOW IN THE CLOUDS, AND IT SHALL BE A SIGN OF THE COVENANT BETWEEN ME AND THE EARTH."

THESE ARE THE FAMILIES OF NOAH'S SONS, SEM, CHAM AND JAPHET. HIS SONS WERE BORN AFTER THE FLOOD. FROM THESE MEN, TNE NATIONS SPREAD ABROAD ON THE EARTH AFTER THE FLOOD.

LOOK AT THIS PLACE! LET US BUILD A CITY HERE!

OK!!!

YES! AND LET US BUILD A TOWER WITH ITS TOP IN THE HEAVENS!

AND LET US MAKE A NAME FOR OURSELVES IN ORDER TO STAY UNITED!

YES!

LET'S DO IT!

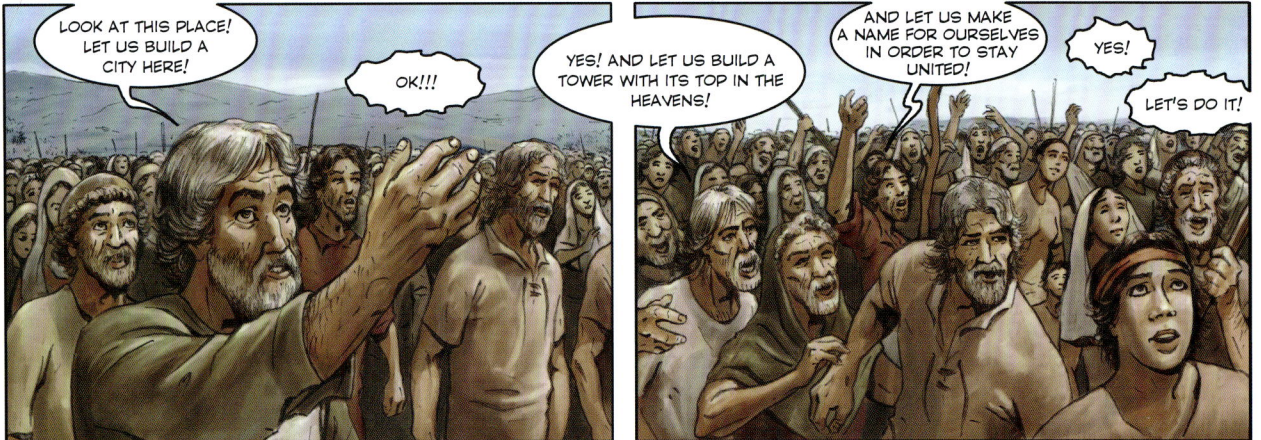

THE LORD CAME DOWN TO SEE THE CITY AND THE TOWER, WHICH THE MORTALS WERE BUILDING.

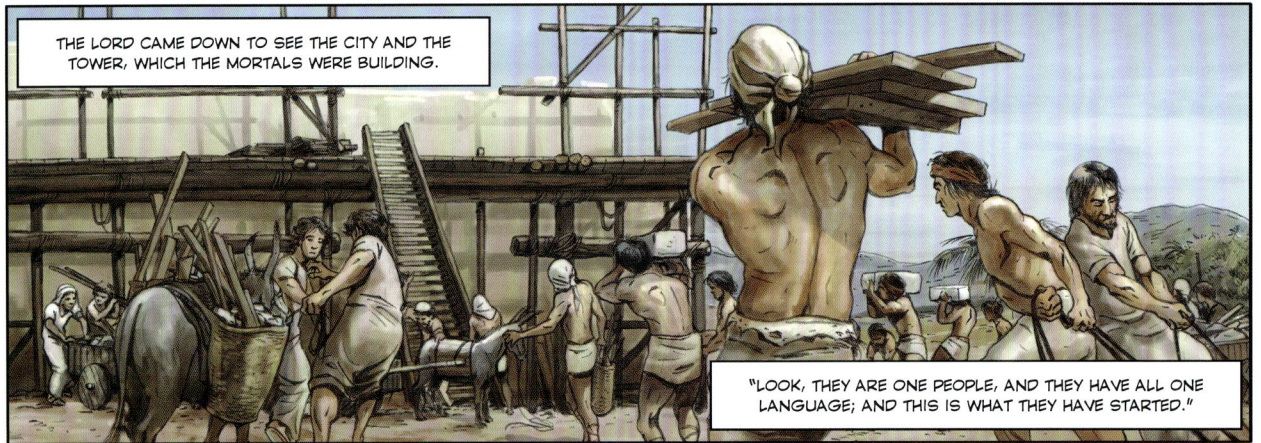

"LOOK, THEY ARE ONE PEOPLE, AND THEY HAVE ALL ONE LANGUAGE; AND THIS IS WHAT THEY HAVE STARTED."

"NOTHING THAT THEY PROPOSE TO DO WILL NOW BE IMPOSSIBLE FOR THEM."

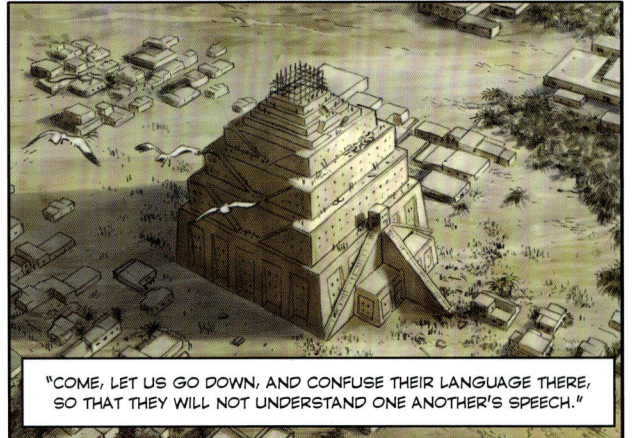

"COME, LET US GO DOWN, AND CONFUSE THEIR LANGUAGE THERE, SO THAT THEY WILL NOT UNDERSTAND ONE ANOTHER'S SPEECH."

SO THE LORD SCATTERED THEM ABROAD FROM THERE OVER THE FACE OF ALL THE EARTH, AND THEY LEFT OFF BUILDING THE CITY.

IT WAS CALLED BABEL.

ABRAM, LOT, AND ABRAM'S WIFE, SARAI, WENT TO CHARAN AND LIVED THERE.

SARAI, I'M GOING FOR A WALK.

OK.

"LEAVE YOUR COUNTRY..."

BUT...

"...AND YOUR KINDRED AND YOUR FATHER'S HOUSE TO THE LAND THAT I WILL SHOW YOU."

"I WILL BLESS THOSE WHO BLESS YOU, AND THE ONE WHO CURSES YOU I WILL CURSE."

"IN YOU ALL THE FAMILIES OF THE EARTH SHALL BE BLESSED!"

SARAI, THE LORD TOLD ME TO LEAVE THIS LAND AND MOVE ELSEWHERE. WE WILL BRING ALL OUR BELONGINGS AND OUR SERVANTS.

LOT, GET READY!

THEY SET FORTH TO GO TO THE LAND OF CANAAN. THERE WAS A FAMINE IN THE LAND. SO ABRAM WENT DOWN TO EGYPT.

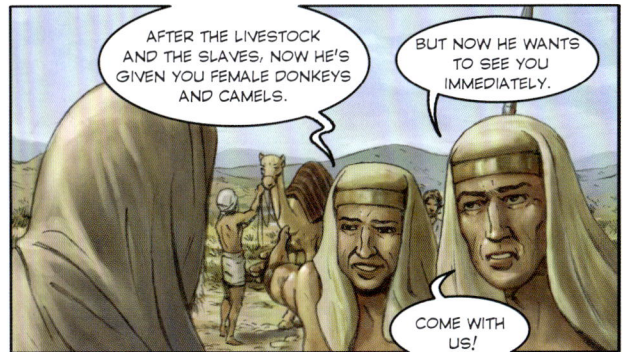

WE'LL SOON BE ARRIVING IN EGYPT. NO ONE MUST KNOW THAT YOU ARE MY WIFE FOR YOU ARE SEDUCTIVE AND I RISK GETTING KILLED AS THEY WOULD WANT YOU FOR THEIR WIFE.

TELL THEM YOU ARE MY SISTER.

VERY WELL.

WHEN ABRAM ENTERED EGYPT THE EGYPTIANS SAW THAT THE WOMAN WAS VERY BEAUTIFUL.

GO, SARAI... DO WHAT HE SAYS!

FOLLOW US!

WE SPOKE ABOUT YOU TO THE PHARAOH. YOU WILL WORK IN HIS HOUSE.

WHAT?!

AND FOR HER SAKE HE DEALT WELL WITH ABRAM.

IT'S US AGAIN, ABRAM!

EVER SINCE YOUR SISTER WORKS FOR HIM, THE PHARAOH IS VERY GENEROUS WITH YOU...

AFTER THE LIVESTOCK AND THE SLAVES, NOW HE'S GIVEN YOU FEMALE DONKEYS AND CAMELS.

BUT NOW HE WANTS TO SEE YOU IMMEDIATELY.

COME WITH US!

*ABRAM IS THE DESCENDANT OF SEM, ONE OF NOAH'S SONS. LOT IS ABRAHAM'S NEPHEW.

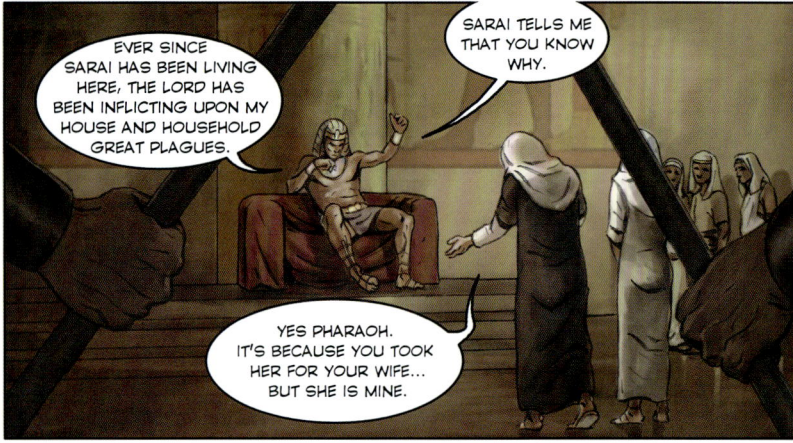

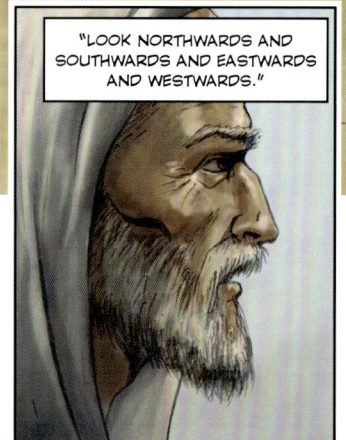

SO ABRAM MOVED HIS TENT, AND CAME AND SETTLED BY THE OAKS OF MAMRE, WHICH ARE AT HEBRON; AND THERE HE BUILT AN ALTAR TO THE LORD.

HEY YOU! TELL ME WHERE I CAN FIND ABRAM. I HAVE AN IMPORTANT MESSAGE!

COME!

EXCUSE US FOR BOTHERING YOU BUT THIS MAN MUST SPEAK TO YOU.

MASTER, THERE WAS A BATTLE THAT CAUSED THE DEFEAT OF THE KINGS OF SODOM AND GOMORRA...

THE VICTORS TOOK THE INHABITANTS OF THESE CITIES AS WELL AS THEIR POSSESSIONS.

LOT IS PRISONER. HE IS THE ONE WHO SENT ME.

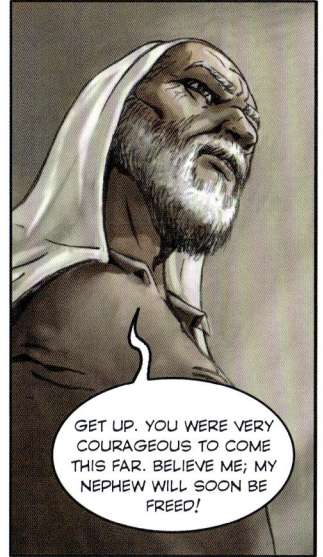

GET UP. YOU WERE VERY COURAGEOUS TO COME THIS FAR. BELIEVE ME; MY NEPHEW WILL SOON BE FREED!

ABRAM ARMED THREE HUNDRED AND EIGHTEEN OF HIS TRAINED MEN, BORN IN HIS HOME. THEN HE BROUGHT BACK ALL THE GOODS, HIS NEPHEW LOT AND THE WOMEN AND THE PEOPLE.

UNCLE, YOU SAVED US. BUT WHAT ARE YOU GOING TO DO WITH ALL THESE PEOPLE?

BRING THEM BACK TO THEIR KINGS.

ABRAM, I, BERA, KING OF SODOM THANK YOU FOR THIS VICTORY.

I, MELCIZEDEK, KING OF SALEM WILL GIVE YOU BREAD AND WINE FOR YOUR MEN AND THOSE THAT YOU FEED.

THANK YOU.

ABRAM, I WILL TAKE THE PEOPLE, BUT TAKE THE GOODS FOR YOURSELF.

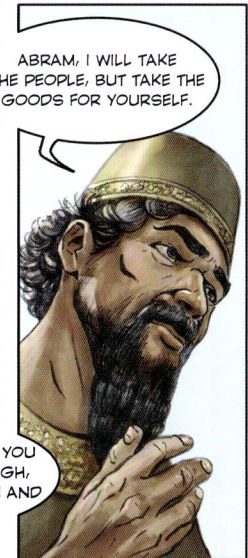

AND BLESSED BE YOU BY GOD MOST HIGH, MAKER OF HEAVEN AND EARTH!

IN THE NAME OF THE LORD, I WILL REFUSE ANYTHING THAT IS YOURS. I WOULDN'T WANT YOU TO SAY, "I HAVE MADE ABRAM RICH."

HOWEVER, MY MEN WILL TAKE THEIR SHARE.

"DO NOT BE AFRAID, ABRAM, I AM YOUR SHIELD; YOUR REWARD SHALL BE VERY GREAT."

BUT, LORD GOD, WHAT WILL YOU GIVE ME?

I CONTINUE CHILDLESS... EVERYTHING I OWN WILL NOT GO TO MY HEIRS.

"NO ONE BUT YOUR VERY OWN ISSUE SHALL BE YOUR HEIR. LOOK TOWARDS HEAVEN..."

"COUNT THE STARS, IF YOU ARE ABLE TO COUNT THEM. SO SHALL YOUR DESCENDANTS BE."

"I AM THE LORD WHO BROUGHT YOU FROM UR OF THE CHALDEANS, TO GIVE YOU THIS LAND TO POSSESS."

HOW AM I TO KNOW THAT I SHALL POSSESS IT?

"BRING ME A HEIFER THREE YEARS OLD, A FEMALE GOAT THREE YEARS OLD, A RAM THREE YEARS OLD, A TURTLE-DOVE, AND A YOUNG PIGEON."

VERY WELL.

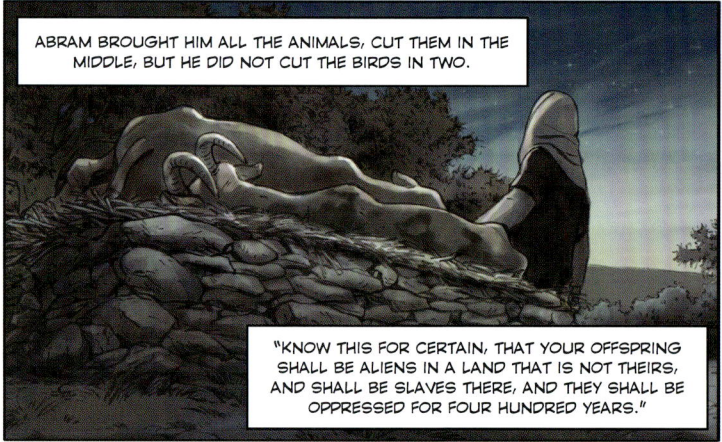

ABRAM BROUGHT HIM ALL THE ANIMALS, CUT THEM IN THE MIDDLE, BUT HE DID NOT CUT THE BIRDS IN TWO.

"KNOW THIS FOR CERTAIN, THAT YOUR OFFSPRING SHALL BE ALIENS IN A LAND THAT IS NOT THEIRS, AND SHALL BE SLAVES THERE, AND THEY SHALL BE OPPRESSED FOR FOUR HUNDRED YEARS."

"BUT I WILL BRING JUDGEMENT ON THE NATION THAT THEY SERVE, AND AFTERWARDS THEY SHALL COME OUT WITH GREAT POSSESSIONS."

"TO YOUR DESCENDANTS I GIVE THIS LAND, FROM THE RIVER OF EGYPT TO THE GREAT RIVER, THE RIVER EUPHRATES."

ON THAT DAY THE LORD MADE A COVENANT WITH ABRAM.

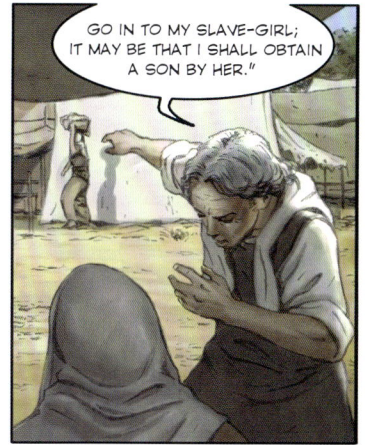

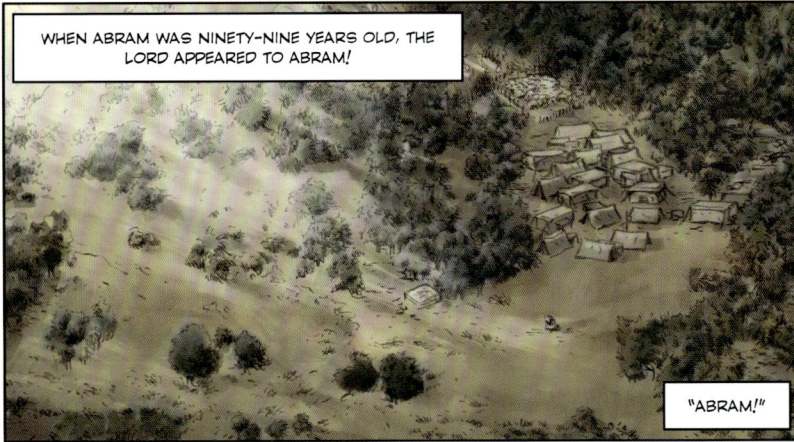

WHEN ABRAM WAS NINETY-NINE YEARS OLD, THE LORD APPEARED TO ABRAM!

"ABRAM!"

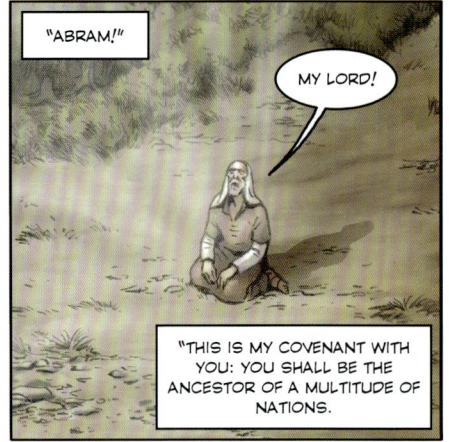

"ABRAM!"

MY LORD!

"THIS IS MY COVENANT WITH YOU: YOU SHALL BE THE ANCESTOR OF A MULTITUDE OF NATIONS.

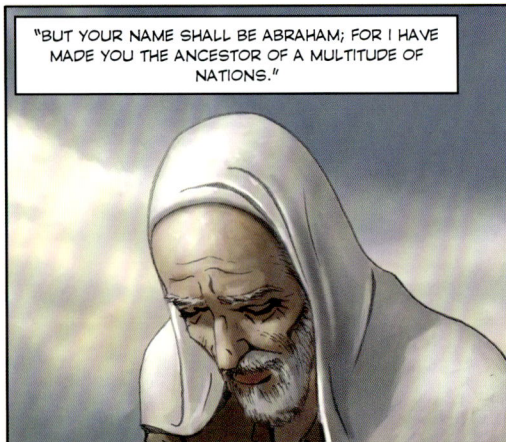

"BUT YOUR NAME SHALL BE ABRAHAM; FOR I HAVE MADE YOU THE ANCESTOR OF A MULTITUDE OF NATIONS."

"I WILL MAKE YOU EXCEEDINGLY FRUITFUL; AND I WILL MAKE NATIONS OF YOU, AND KINGS SHALL COME FROM YOU. I WILL ESTABLISH MY COVENANT BETWEEN ME AND YOU, AND IT WILL BE AN EVERLASTING COVENANT."

"THIS IS MY COVENANT. WHEN HE IS EIGHT DAYS OLD, EVERY MALE SHALL BE CIRCUMCISED."

"YOU SHALL NOT CALL YOUR WIFE SARAI, BUT SARAH SHALL BE HER NAME."

"I WILL BLESS HER, AND SHE SHALL GIVE RISE TO NATIONS; KINGS OF PEOPLE SHALL COME FROM HER."

HOW CAN A CHILD BE BORN TO A MAN WHO IS A HUNDRED YEARS OLD AND A WOMAN WHO IS NINETY?

ISHMAEL IS OUR ONLY SON...

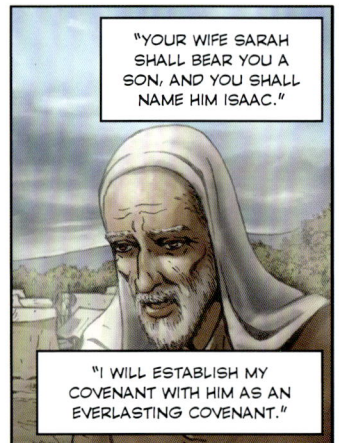

"YOUR WIFE SARAH SHALL BEAR YOU A SON, AND YOU SHALL NAME HIM ISAAC."

"I WILL ESTABLISH MY COVENANT WITH HIM AS AN EVERLASTING COVENANT."

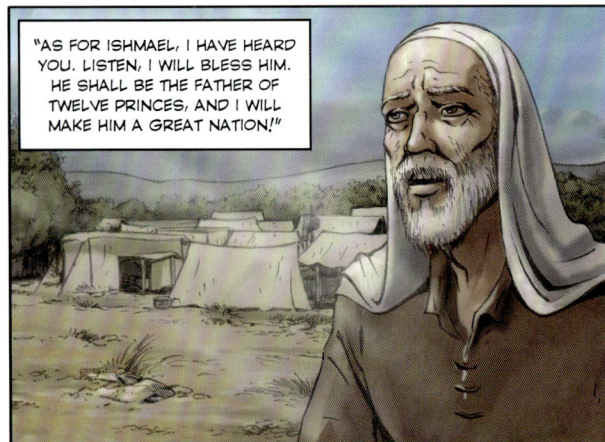

"AS FOR ISHMAEL, I HAVE HEARD YOU. LISTEN, I WILL BLESS HIM. HE SHALL BE THE FATHER OF TWELVE PRINCES, AND I WILL MAKE HIM A GREAT NATION!"

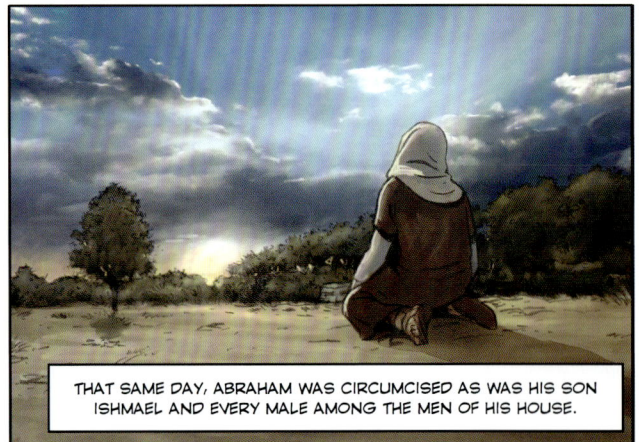

THAT SAME DAY, ABRAHAM WAS CIRCUMCISED AS WAS HIS SON ISHMAEL AND EVERY MALE AMONG THE MEN OF HIS HOUSE.

ABRAHAM WAS SITTING AT THE ENTRANCE OF HIS TENT. THE LORD APPEARED BY THE OAKS OF MAMRE.

MY LORDS!

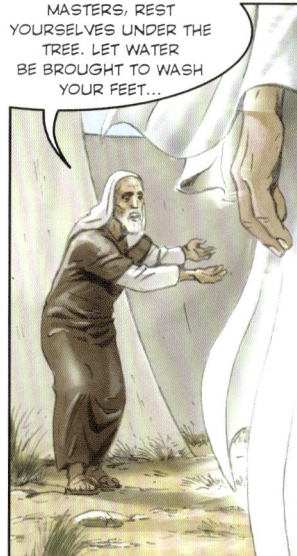

MASTERS, REST YOURSELVES UNDER THE TREE. LET WATER BE BROUGHT TO WASH YOUR FEET...

... AND I WILL FEED YOU!

VERY WELL, WE ACCEPT YOUR INVITATION.

SARAH?

SHE'S IN THE TENT.

WHERE IS YOUR WIFE, SARAH?

LET ME TELL YOU THAT IN ONE YEAR, I WILL RETURN...

... AND SARAH SHALL HAVE A SON!

A SON? HOW COULD ELDERS SUCH AS OURSELVES HAVE A CHILD?

HA HA HA!

WHY ARE YOU LAUGHING, SARAH?

IS ANYTHING TOO WONDERFUL FOR THE LORD?

I DID NOT LAUGH, LORD!

YES, YOU DID LAUGH.

WHATEVER YOU MAY THINK, YOU WILL HAVE A SON!

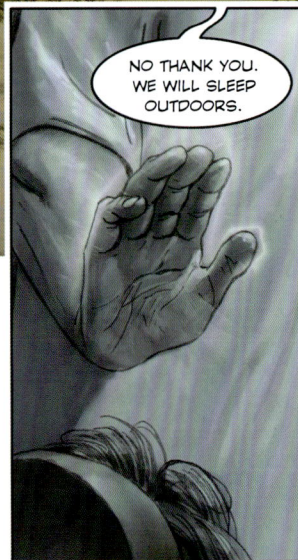

THE SUN WAS RISING ON THE EARTH. THEN THE LORD RAINED ON SODOM AND GOMORRAH SULPHUR AND FIRE FROM THE LORD OUT OF HEAVEN; AND HE OVERTHREW THOSE CITIES, AND ALL THE PLAIN, AND ALL THE INHABITANTS OF THE CITIES, AND WHAT GREW ON THE GROUND.

LOT'S WIFE LOOKED BACK, AND BECAME A PILLAR OF SALT.

ABRAHAM WENT EARLY IN THE MORNING TO THE PLACE WHERE HE HAD STOOD BEFORE THE LORD. HE LOOKED DOWN TOWARDS SODOM AND GOMORRAH AND TOWARDS ALL THE LAND OF THE PLAIN, AND SAW THE SMOKE OF THE LAND GOING UP LIKE THE SMOKE OF A FURNACE.

WHEN GOD DESTROYED THE CITIES OF THE PLAIN, HE REMEMBERED ABRAHAM, AND SENT LOT OUT OF THE MIDST OF THE OVERTHROW.

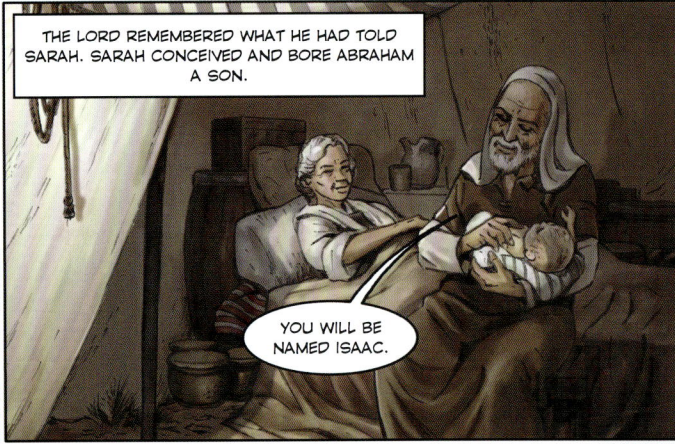

THE LORD REMEMBERED WHAT HE HAD TOLD SARAH. SARAH CONCEIVED AND BORE ABRAHAM A SON.

YOU WILL BE NAMED ISAAC.

AND ABRAHAM CIRCUMCISED HIS SON ISAAC WHEN HE WAS EIGHT DAYS OLD, AS GOD HAD COMMANDED HIM.

WHEN THE LORD TOLD ME THAT I WOULD HAVE A CHILD, I HAD A GOOD LAUGH. YET, NOW I AM NURSING MY SON.

THE CHILD GREW AND ABRAHAM MADE A GREAT FEAST ON THE DAY THAT ISAAC WAS WEANED.

YES BUT I CAN'T STAND THAT HE'S PLAYING WITH THE OTHER ONE.

LOOK HOW SWIFT OUR SON IS!

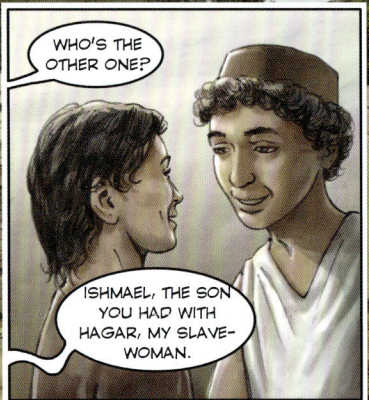

WHO'S THE OTHER ONE?

ISHMAEL, THE SON YOU HAD WITH HAGAR, MY SLAVE-WOMAN.

MY SON MUST BE THE ONLY ONE TO INHERIT. CAST HIM OUT!

BUT THAT'S IMPOSSIBLE, HE'S ALSO MY SON!

"WHATEVER SARAH SAYS TO YOU, DO AS SHE TELLS YOU, FOR IT IS THROUGH ISAAC THAT OFFSPRING SHALL BE NAMED AFTER YOU."

ABRAHAM TOOK BREAD AND A SKIN OF WATER, AND GAVE IT TO HAGAR. HE ALSO GAVE HER THE BOY AND SENT HER AWAY.

I AM LOST AND WE ARE OUT OF WATER. I HAVE NO CHOICE BUT TO LEAVE YOU HERE.

"WHAT TROUBLES YOU, HAGAR? DO NOT BE AFRAID; FOR GOD HAS HEARD THE VOICE OF THE BOY WHERE HE IS."

A WELL?

SHE WENT AND FILLED THE SKIN WITH WATER, AND GAVE THE BOY A DRINK. GOD WAS WITH THE BOY, AND HE GREW UP; HE LIVED IN THE WILDERNESS, AND BECAME AN EXPERT WITH THE BOW. HIS MOTHER GOT A WIFE FOR HIM FROM THE LAND OF EGYPT.

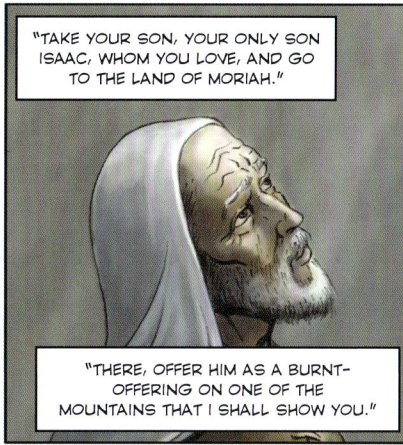

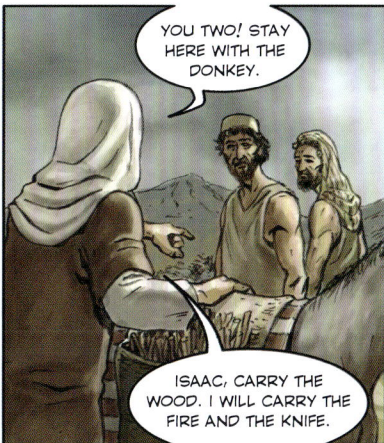

THE ANGEL OF THE LORD CALLED TO HIM FROM HEAVEN.

"ABRAHAM, ABRAHAM!"

SARAH LIVED FOR ONE HUNDRED AND TWENTY SEVEN YEARS. SARAH DIED IN HEBRON, IN THE LAND OF CANAAN.

I AM BUT A STRANGER AMONG YOU, SON OF HETH. BUT GIVE ME PROPERTY FOR A BURYING PLACE, SO THAT I MAY BURY SARAH.

MY LORD; YOU ARE A PRINCE OF GOD AMONG US.

BURY YOUR WIFE WHERE YOU WISH. NONE OF US WILL STOP YOU.

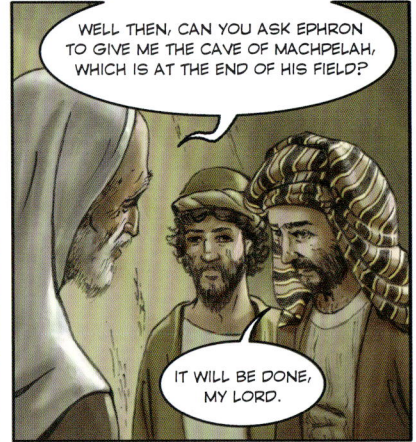

WELL THEN, CAN YOU ASK EPHRON TO GIVE ME THE CAVE OF MACHPELAH, WHICH IS AT THE END OF HIS FIELD?

IT WILL BE DONE, MY LORD.

ABRAHAM, I, EPHRON, GIVE YOU THE FIELD, AND I GIVE YOU THE CAVE!

THE SONS OF MY PEOPLE ARE MY WITNESSES. YOU CAN BURY YOUR WIFE THERE.

THANK YOU EPHRON BUT ACCEPT THAT I PAY FOR THE FIELD.

LISTEN, MY LORD, A PIECE OF LAND WORTH FOUR HUNDRED SHEKELS OF SILVER- WHAT IS THAT BETWEEN YOU AND ME?

I INSIST. THIS IS WHAT I OWE YOU.

THE FIELD OF EPHRON IN MACHPELAH, THE FIELD AND THE CAVE THUS BECAME ABRAHAM'S, IN THE EYES OF THE SONS OF HETH. ABRAHAM BURIED SARAH, HIS WIFE, IN THE CAVE.

YOU ARE MY OLDEST AND MOST FAITHFUL SERVANT. YOU KNOW THAT I AM OLD.

YOU ARE THE ONLY ONE I CAN ASK.

PUT YOUR HAND UNDER MY THIGH AND I WILL MAKE YOU SWEAR BY THE LORD, THE GOD OF HEAVEN AND EARTH, THAT YOU WILL NOT GET A WIFE FOR MY SON FROM THE WOMEN HERE.

GO TO MY COUNTRY AND GET HIM A WIFE.

I SWEAR, MY LORD.

THE SERVENT TOOK TEN OF HIS MASTER'S CAMELS AND SET OUT TO MESOPOTAMIA, TO THE CITY OF NAHOR.

O LORD, GOD OF MY MASTER ABRAHAM, LET THE GIRL WHO WILL LET ME DRINK FROM HER JAR AND WILL GIVE WATER TO MY CAMELS BE THAT ONE TO THAT YOU HAVE APPOINTED FOR ISAAC.

A YOUNG GIRL WENT DOWN TO THE SPRING AND FILLED HER JAR. THE SERVANT RAN TO MEET HER. SHE QUICKLY GAVE HIM A DRINK.

I WILL DRAW SOME FOR YOUR CAMELS ALSO. THEY MUST BE THIRSTY.

THANK YOU FOR THE FRESH WATER!

HERE IS A RING AND TWO BRACELETS TO THANK YOU.

OH, MASTER!

THOSE JEWELS LOOK MARVELOUS ON YOU!

WHO ARE YOU?

I AM REBECCA, DAUGHTER OF BETHUEL, SON OF MILCA AND NACHOR*.

DO YOU THINK I COULD SPEND THE NIGHT AT YOUR FATHER'S HOUSE?

OF COURSE, MASTER! THERE IS ROOM FOR YOU AND EVEN FOR THE CAMELS.

BLESSED BE THE LORD, THE GOD OF MY MASTER ABRAHAM, WHO HAS NOT FORSAKEN HIS FAITHFULNESS TOWARDS MY MASTER.

AS FOR ME, THE LORD HAS LED ME ON THE WAY TO THE HOUSE OF MY MASTER'S KIN.

THE GIRL RAN AND TOLD HER MOTHER'S HOUSEHOLD ABOUT THESE THINGS. REBECCA HAD A BROTHER WHOSE NAME WAS LABAN. HE HAD SEEN THE RING AND THE BRACELETS ON HIS SISTER'S ARMS. SO HE WENT TO THE MAN.

THIS IS MY BROTHER, LABAN.

COME IN, O BLESSED OF THE LORD!

WHY DO YOU STAND OUTSIDE? I HAVE PREPARED A PLACE FOR YOU, YOUR MEN AND ANIMALS.

WELCOME!

SIT DOWN AND EAT.

THANK YOU BUT I WILL NOT EAT UNTIL I HAVE TOLD MY ERRAND.

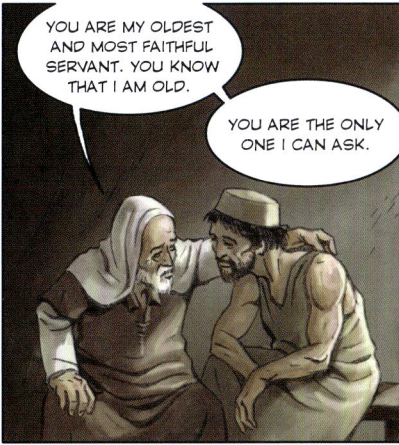

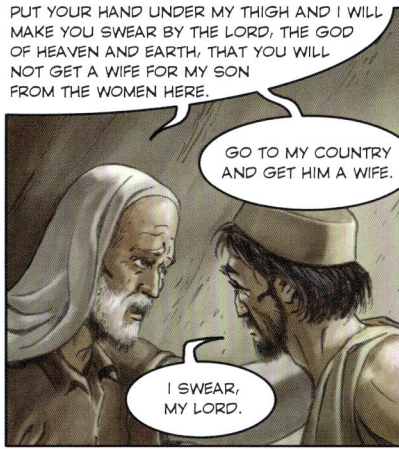

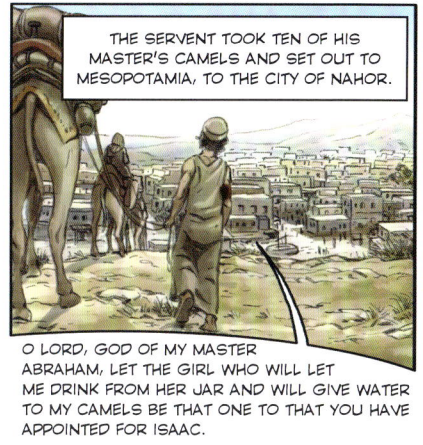

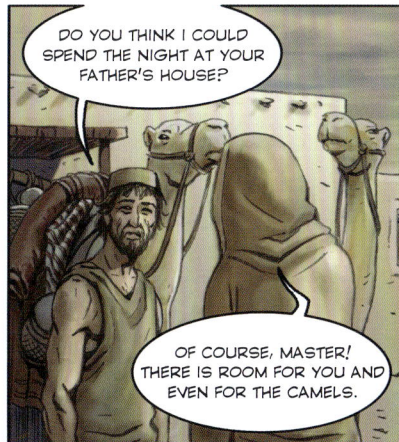

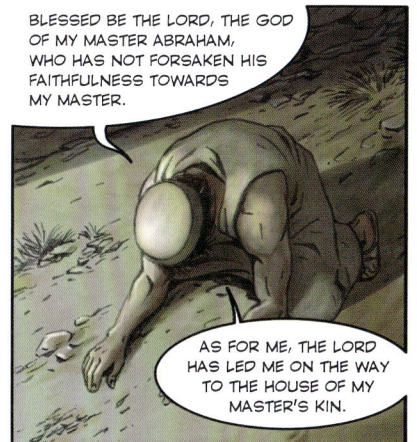

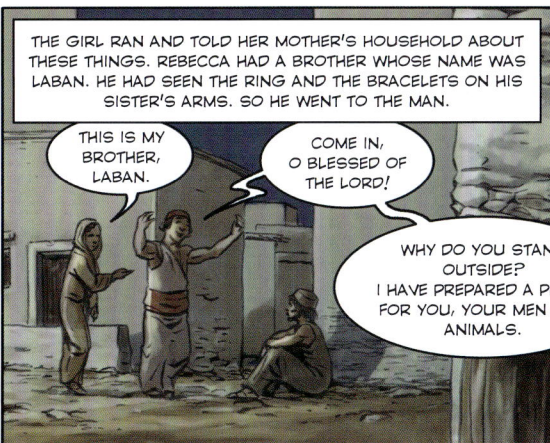

*NACHOR IS ABRAHAM'S BROTHER.

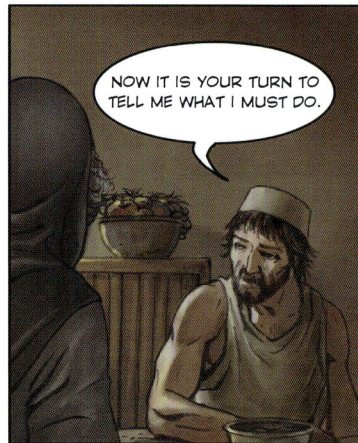

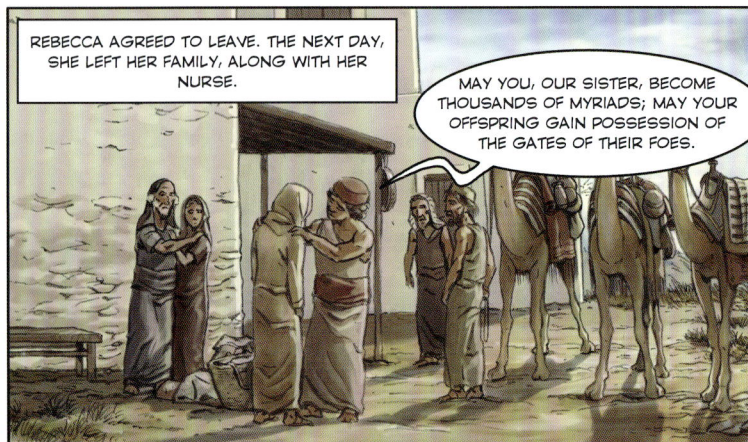

ISAAC, I GAVE GIFTS TO THE SONS OF MY CONCUBINES THAT I SENT AWAY FROM YOU.

BUT IT IS TO YOU, MY SON, THAT I LEFT EVERYTHING I OWN.

FATHER!!

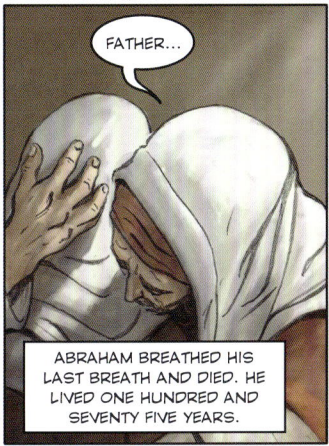

FATHER...

ABRAHAM BREATHED HIS LAST BREATH AND DIED. HE LIVED ONE HUNDRED AND SEVENTY FIVE YEARS.

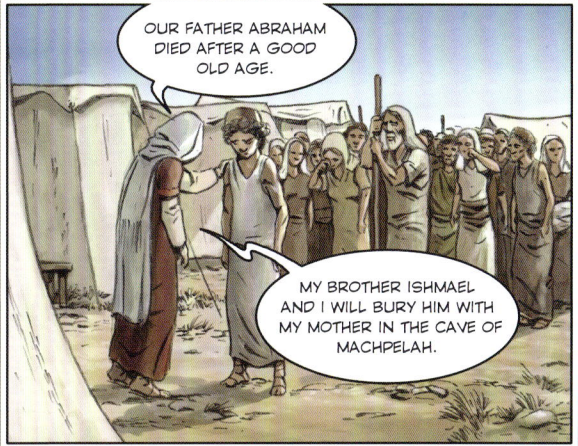

OUR FATHER ABRAHAM DIED AFTER A GOOD OLD AGE.

MY BROTHER ISHMAEL AND I WILL BURY HIM WITH MY MOTHER IN THE CAVE OF MACHPELAH.

AFTER THE DEATH OF ABRAHAM GOD BLESSED HIS SON ISAAC.

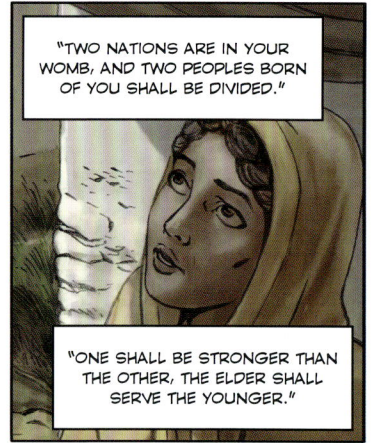

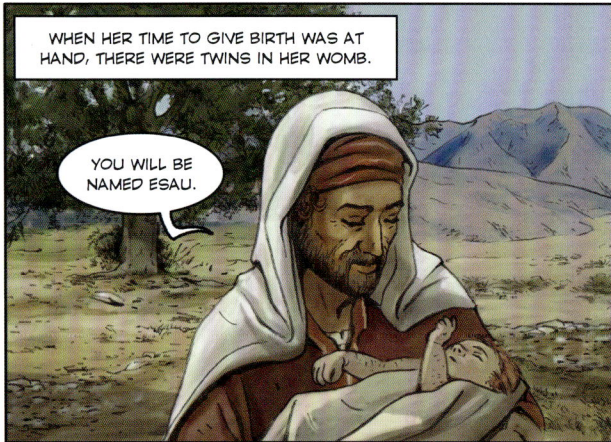

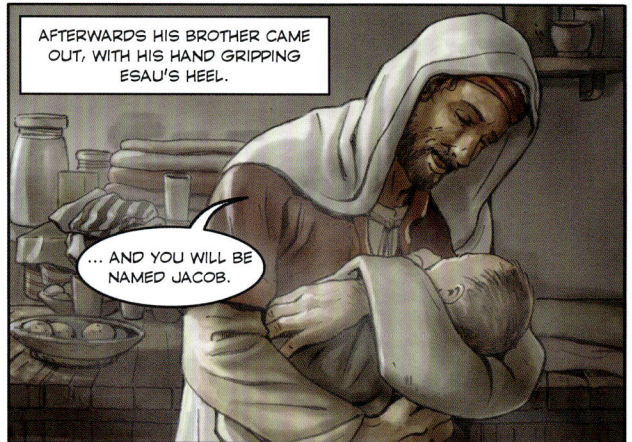

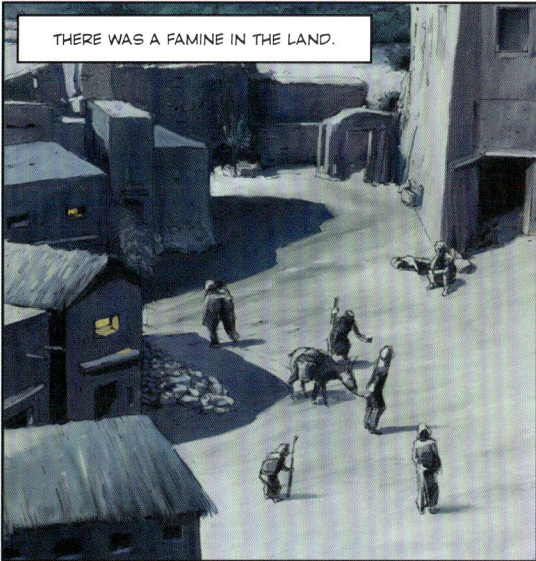

THERE WAS A FAMINE IN THE LAND.

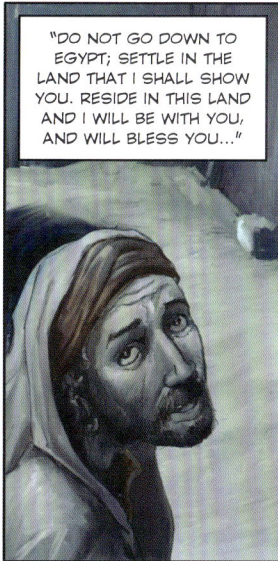

"DO NOT GO DOWN TO EGYPT; SETTLE IN THE LAND THAT I SHALL SHOW YOU. RESIDE IN THIS LAND AND I WILL BE WITH YOU, AND WILL BLESS YOU..."

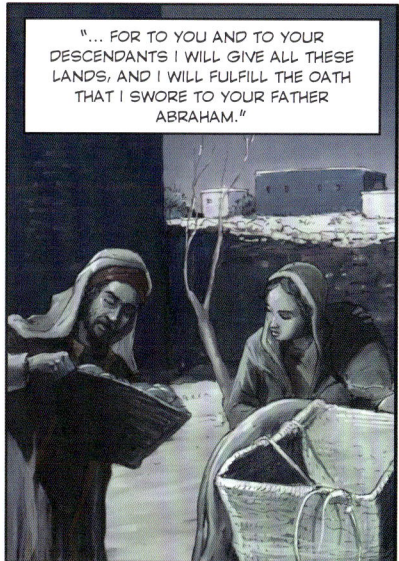

"... FOR TO YOU AND TO YOUR DESCENDANTS I WILL GIVE ALL THESE LANDS, AND I WILL FULFILL THE OATH THAT I SWORE TO YOUR FATHER ABRAHAM."

"I WILL MAKE YOUR OFFSPRING AS NUMEROUS AS THE STARS OF HEAVEN, AND WILL GIVE TO YOUR OFFSPRING ALL THESE LANDS; AND ALL THE NATIONS OF THE EARTH SHALL GAIN BLESSING FOR THEMSELVES THROUGH YOUR OFFSPRING."

ISAAC SETTLED IN GERAR.

ISAAC!

WHAT DO YOU WANT MY FRIEND?

TELL ME, WHO IS THAT BEAUTIFUL WOMAN WITH YOU?

SHE IS MY SISTER.

WHY DIDN'T YOU ADMIT THAT YOU WERE MY HUSBAND?

REBECCA, IF THEY FIND OUT, THEY WILL KILL ME AND TAKE YOU AS THEIR WIFE.

WE MUST BE CAUTIOUS.

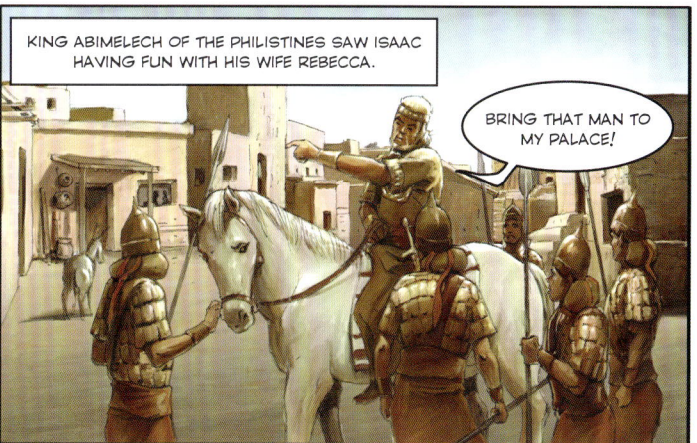

KING ABIMELECH OF THE PHILISTINES SAW ISAAC HAVING FUN WITH HIS WIFE REBECCA.

BRING THAT MAN TO MY PALACE!

ISAAC DEPARTED FROM THERE AND CAMPED IN THE VALLEY OF GERAR AND SETTLED THERE.

THIS WELL THAT WE HAVE JUST BUILT WILL BE CALLED REHOBOTH. THE LORD HAS ALLOWED US TO SETTLE HERE AND PROSPER IN THIS LAND.

"I AM THE GOD OF YOUR FATHER ABRAHAM; DO NOT BE AFRAID, FOR I AM WITH YOU."

HE BUILT AN ALTAR THERE, CALLED ON THE NAME OF THE LORD, AND PITCHED HIS TENT THERE. AND THERE ISAAC'S SERVANTS DUG A WELL.

KING ABIMELECH, WHAT ARE YOU DOING HERE? YOU CHASED ME AWAY FROM GERAR...

WE MUST RECOGNIZE THAT THE LORD IS WITH YOU. LET US MAKE A COVENANT WITH YOU. LET'S MAKE AN OATH THAT WE WILL NEVER HARM EACH OTHER.

GREAT! LET US CELEBRATE!

ISAAC MADE THEM A FEAST. IN THE MORNING THEY ROSE EARLY AND EXCHANGED OATHS; AND ISAAC SET THEM ON THEIR WAY, AND THEY DEPARTED FROM HIM IN PEACE.

WE WILL CALL THIS WELL SCHIBAH AND THIS PLACE BEER-SCHEBA.

ISAAC WAS GETTING OLD AND HIS EYES WERE SO WEAK THAT HE COULD NOT SEE. SO HE CALLED HIS ELDER SON ESAU.

ESAU, MY SON, ARE YOU THERE?

YES, FATHER, HERE I AM.

I HAVE BECOME OLD. I MUST BLESS YOU BEFORE GOD BEFORE I DIE...

IN ORDER TO DO THAT, YOU MUST HUNT GAME AND PREPARE FOR ME THE SAVORY FOOD THAT I LIKE AND THAT I WILL EAT.

YES, FATHER.

JACOB, YOUR FATHER WISHES TO BLESS YOUR BROTHER BEFORE HE DIES BUT I WANT HIM TO BLESS YOU.

MOTHER! BUT THAT'S IMPOSSIBLE!!

BE QUIET! I WILL PREPARE THE FOOD FOR YOUR FATHER AND YOU WILL BRING IT TO HIM.

AND SO, I WILL BE BLESSED INSTEAD OF MY BROTHER...

BUT IF MY FATHER TOUCHES ME, HE WILL FEEL THAT I AM NOT AS HAIRY AS ESAU.

IF HE DISCOVERS THAT I HAVE BETRAYED HIM, HE WILL CURSE ME!

DON'T WORRY, JACOB. GO AND GET SOME DEER AND LET ME TAKE CARE OF IT.

IF THERE IS A CURSE, IT WILL BE ON ME.

REBECCA TOOK THE GARMENTS OF HER ELDER SON ESAU, THE BEST ONES IN THE HOUSE AND SHE HANDED THEM TO JACOB, HER YOUNGEST SON.

SHE PUT THE SKINS OF THE KIDS ON HIS HANDS AND ON THE SMOOTH PART OF HIS NECK.

NOW YOU ARE READY. BRING THE FOOD AND BREAD TO YOUR FATHER.

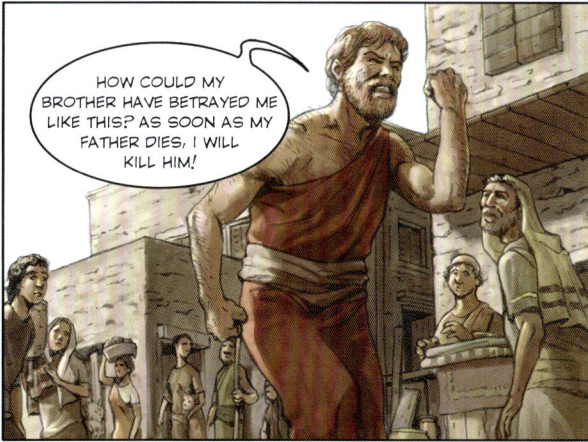

HOW COULD MY BROTHER HAVE BETRAYED ME LIKE THIS? AS SOON AS MY FATHER DIES, I WILL KILL HIM!

THE WORDS OF ESAU WERE TOLD TO REBECCA.

JACOB, YOUR BROTHER WANTS REVENGE BY KILLING YOU. GO TO MY BROTHER LABAN'S HOME. YOU WILL BE ALLOWED TO LIVE THERE FOR SOME TIME. UNTIL THEN, ESAU MIGHT HAVE FORGIVEN YOU.

YOU WILL MARRY ONE OF THE DAUGHTERS OF LABAN. MAY GOD BLESS YOU AND MAKE YOU FRUITFUL. MAY HE GIVE TO YOU AND YOUR OFFSPRING THE BLESSING OF ABRAHAM.

YOU WILL BE MASTER OF THE LAND THAT GOD GAVE HIM.

NOW, GO!

"I AM THE LORD, THE GOD OF ABRAHAM YOUR FATHER AND THE GOD OF ISAAC; THE LAND ON WHICH YOU LIE I WILL GIVE TO YOU AND TO YOUR OFFSPRING."

"YOUR OFFSPRING WILL BE LIKE THE DUST OF THE EARTH. YOU SHALL SPREAD ABROAD TO THE WEST AND TO THE EAST AND TO THE NORTH AND TO THE SOUTH; AND ALL THE FAMILIES OF THE EARTH SHALL BE BLESSED IN YOU AND IN YOUR OFFSPRING."

"KNOW THAT I AM WITH YOU AND WILL KEEP YOU WHEREVER YOU GO, AND WILL BRING YOU BACK TO THIS LAND; FOR I WILL NOT LEAVE YOU UNTIL I HAVE DONE WHAT I HAVE PROMISED YOU."

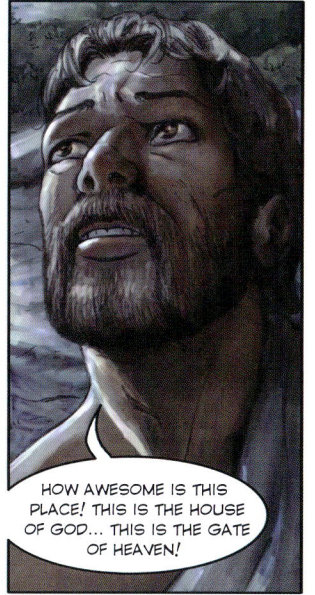

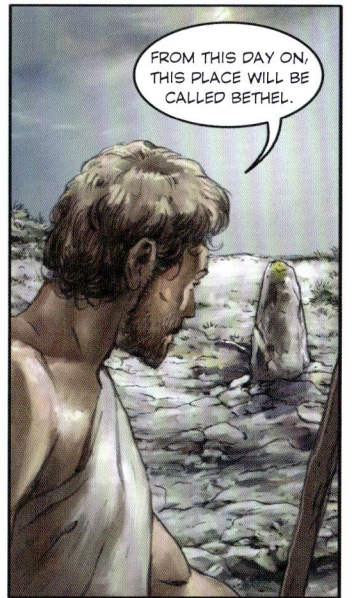

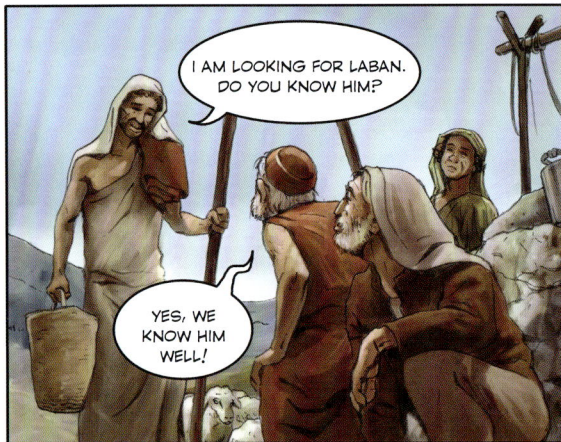

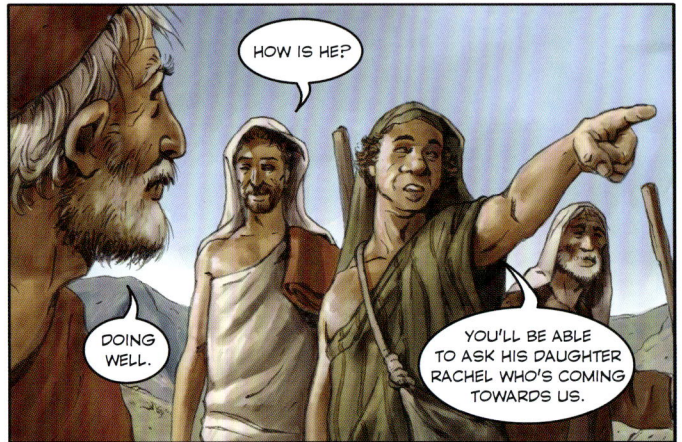

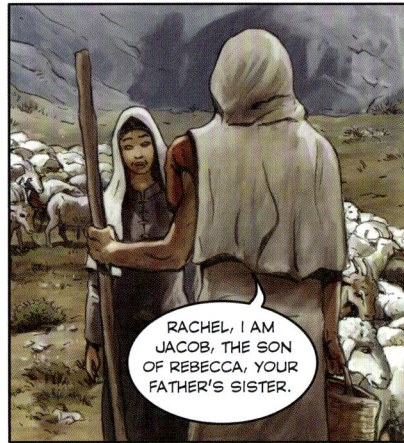

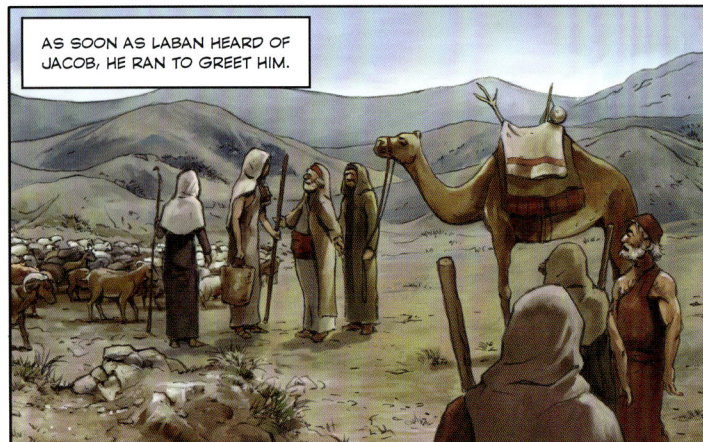

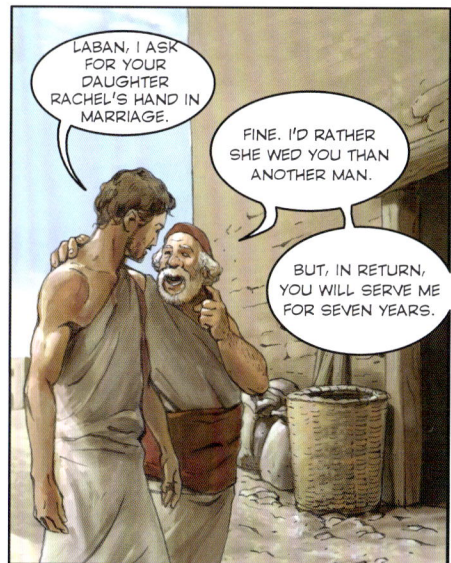

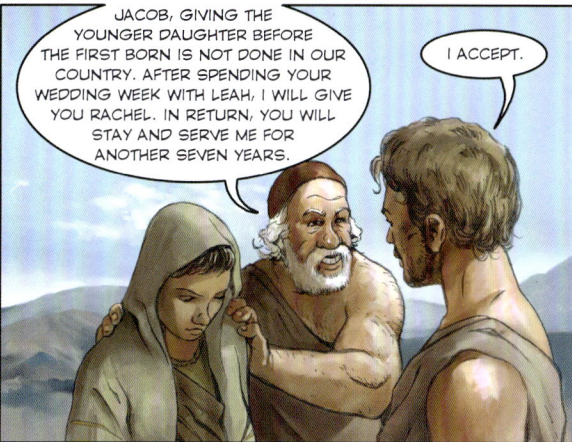

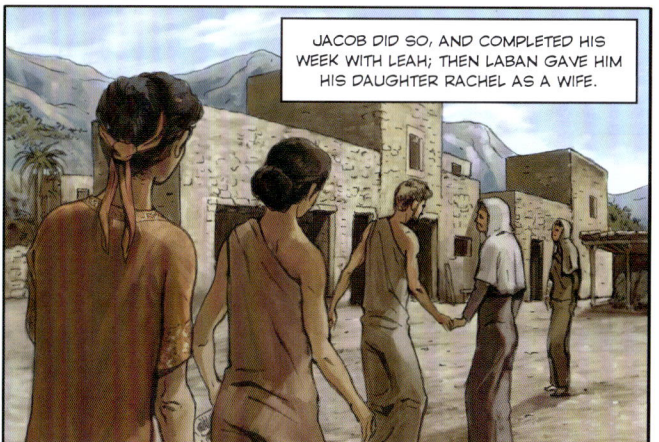

THE LORD SAW THAT LEAH WAS UNLOVED SO HE OPENED HER WOMB WHILE RACHEL WAS BARREN.
LEAH CONCEIVED* AND BORE A SON THAT SHE NAMED REUBEN.

WHEN RACHEL SAW THAT SHE BORE JACOB NO
CHILDREN, SHE ENVIED HER SISTER. SHE GAVE HIM
HER MAID BILHAH** AS A WIFE; BILHAH CONCEIVED AND
BORE JACOB A SON.

LEAH, REALIZING THAT SHE HAD CEASED BEARING CHILDREN, TOOK HER MAID ZILPAH AND
GAVE HER TO JACOB AS A WIFE. ZILPAH*** BORE JACOB A SON.

GOD REMEMBERED RACHEL AND HEEDED HER BY OPENING HER WOMB. SHE
CONCEIVED AND BORE A SON. SHE NAMED HIS JOSEPH.

*LEAH HAD SIX SONS: REUBEN, SIMON, LEVI, JUDDAH, ISSAKAR, ZABULON AND A DAUGHTER, DINE. **BILHAH HAD TWO SONS, DAN AND NEPHTAU.
**ZILPAH HAD TWO SONS, GAD AND ASHER.

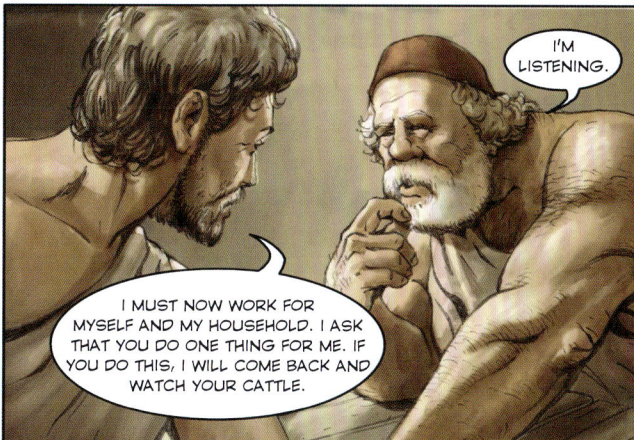

SO, THE ANGEL TOLD ME: "JACOB, I SAW WHAT LABAN DID TO YOU. I AM THE GOD FOR WHOM YOU ANOINTED A PILLAR AT BETHEL. NOW LEAVE THIS LAND AND RETURN TO THE LAND OF YOUR BIRTH."

THERE, NOW YOU HAVE HEARD THE MESSAGE THAT WAS GIVEN TO ME.

NOW THAT I HAVE BECOME RICH, LABAN AND YOUR BROTHERS THINK THAT I STOLE FROM THEM BUT IT IS YOUR FATHER WHO HAS TRICKED ME MANY TIMES.

WE MUST LEAVE!!

HE ALSO PLAYED US FOR FOOLS!

HE SOLD US AND WE HAVE NOTHING. ALL THE RICHES THAT WE HAVE OBTAINED THROUGH YOUR GOD BELONG TO US AND TO OUR CHILDREN!

LET US DO WHAT GOD TOLD YOU.

LET'S LEAVE!

WHILE LABAN HAD GONE TO SHEAR HIS SHEEP, RACHEL STOLE HER FATHER'S HOUSEHOLD GOODS.

JACOB FLED WITH ALL THAT HE HAD; HE CROSSED THE RIVER AND SET OUT TOWARDS THE HILL COUNTRY OF GILEAD.

ON THE THIRD DAY, LABAN WAS TOLD THAT JACOB HAD FLED. HE TOOK HIS KINSFOLK WITH HIM AND PURSUED HIM FOR SEVEN DAYS...

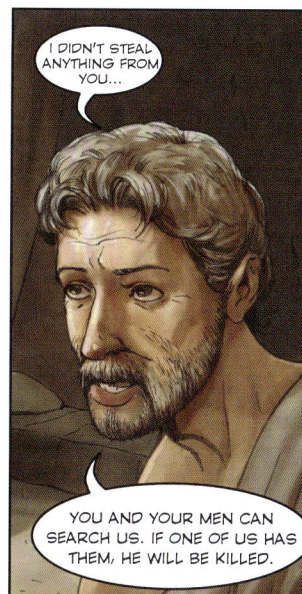

JACOB, LET'S PUT AN END TO THESE QUARRELS. LET'S MAKE A COVENANT, YOU AND I. LET IT BE A WITNESS BETWEEN US.
MAY THIS HEAP OF STONE AND THIS PILLAR BE OUR WITNESSES THAT THE LORD WATCHES OVER YOU AND ME WHEN WE ARE ABSENT ONE FROM THE OTHER. IF YOU MISTREAT MY DAUGHTERS OR TAKE OTHER WIVES, GOD WILL BE A WITNESS TO IT.
AND I SWEAR NOT TO PASS IN YOUR DIRECTION FOR FEAR OF HARM.
I SWEAR NOT TO PASS THIS PLACE IN YOUR DIRECTION.
LABAN NAMED THE SACRED SPOT JEGAR SAHADUTHA AND JACOB NAMED IT GALED. JACOB HELD A BURNT OFFERING ON THE MOUNTAIN AND INVITED ALL THE MEN TO DINE WITH HIM. SO, THEY ATE AND SPENT THE NIGHT ON THE MOUNTAIN. EARLY IN THE MORNING LABAN ROSE UP, AND KISSED HIS GRANDCHILDREN AND HIS DAUGHTERS AND BLESSED THEM; THEN HE DEPARTED AND RETURNED HOME.
THE END.